Fall Ill
Medicine

poems by

Carrie Seitzinger

Fall Ill
Medicine

SMALL DOGGIES PRESS

a division of

SMALL DOGGIES OMNIMEDIA

Portland, Oregon

SMALL DOGGIES PRESS

a division of Small Doggies Omnimedia

⋘ smalldoggiesomnimedia.com ⋙

Fall Ill Medicine
poems by Carrie Seitzinger

SMALL DOGGIES PRESS© 2012
1ST PRINTING.

ISBN 978-0-9848744-1-5

PRINTED IN THE UNITED STATES OF AMERICA
10 • 9 • 8 • 7 • 6 • 5 • 4 • 3 • 2 • 1

Small Doggies trade paperback edition, July 2012

Small Doggies Press: *WWW.SMALLDOGGIESPRESS.COM*

Carrie Seitzinger: *WWW.CARRIESEITZINGER.COM*

Cover Design by *Andrew Farris.*
Interior Layout by *Andrew Farris.*
Edited by *Matty Byloos, Maggie Foree, & Maggie Wells.*
Type set in Chaparral *& Hoefler Text Black Swash*

Previously Published

Thank you to the following publications where
poems from this manuscript first appeared.

Cobalt Poets
DASH
Don't Blame the Ugly Mug (Tebot Bach, 2011)
Housefire
Mosaic
Nouns of Assemblage (Housefire, 2011)
Poor Claudia
Small Doggies Magazine
Sparkle & Blink
The People's Apocalypse (Lit Star Press, 2012)
Unshod Quills

Fall Ill Medicine
Poems by Carrie Seitzinger

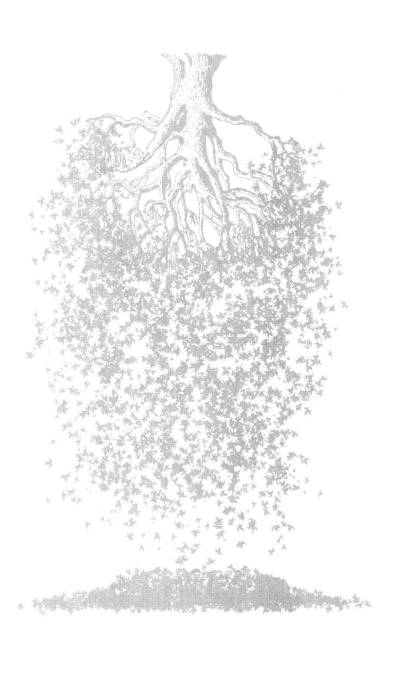

Secret Pages I

This is the way the summer lulls us,
heat to sleep, heat to sleep—
but where was my body last night?

Let me hold it in the palm of your bed.

There, I am weakened
to a pool of ghostcolor,
and the slick crows stop following me
like a rain cloud, and bid no omen at all.

Hold my navel under your tongue
if you think you want to speak to my center.
My body will dissolve like a disk of communion,
my body is the flesh of any body.

Hold my neck like a guitar.

Hand me my gift of the Holy Spirit
if it comes in a pen case.
Hand me my gift of the wholly spirit.

And we will bite each other's tongues,
and keep our secrets secret.

Chair

I.

A lover tied me to a chair once.
I like the memory of it
more than the act itself.

II.

I left the idea of you in Virginia
with our phone sex and all of the mosquitoes
who adored my blood.
I can't remember your voice
saying what I want to remember it saying,
but everything else.

III.

Now that I am a lesbian, every time
I see a woman I think of sex. I imagine
the texture of her hair. I imagine if
she would laugh with me in the
morning. I wake up in a good mood
when I am sure about something.

IV.

I made love to a chair once.
It was equal and homosexual:
my ankles to the legs,
my arms to its arms.
And afterwards,
wishing for someone
to make themselves comfortable
inside me.

One Step Closer (It's the Light)

It's the Earth cracking like there's a sun inside.
The world we've learned through fingers,
every uncaught moment, releases.

It's the voices outside the window that rise
into the night sky like detached spidernets.
It's the crumbs on the kitchen floor that dirty our feet.
It's the teacher who watches his students
go on with summer and looks down
as he tells them they were good.
It's the elderly woman who never lost the crystal viridian
around her pupils, but is starting to forget
where she keeps the bread.
It's your father's whole story
told in a bar, that slowly breaks off
into the ocean, like all good stories do.
It's the dream that woke you up and made you cry
and made you too scared to fall back into your mind.
It's the house that your lovelies built
around themselves and you,
a house with wood that wouldn't give.

If you step closer to the nearest star,
your eyes will go dead like dashboard lights.
Invent a new color for the occasion.
One step closer and your red skull turns black.
Your hands will turn to loose cobwebs
in the heat of what is Real.
You almost got lost in that cave, the shadows
moved on the wall like someone's lost allegory.

Out here your hair singes out of its tangles
like dynamite wicks.
You could've sworn your skull was white.
One step closer and you'll find the birds
have borrowed your hands for their nests.

Write your moon because it swings overhead
like a fishing pole buoy.
Write your blood because it slips away from your body
whether you like it or not.
Write your streets because they howl a melody
full of strange lights.
One step closer and you'll remember the tune.
The light will cradle your head like a madman's.
It's the light in the room that makes you cry
whether or not something sad
or beautiful has happened.

The light throws down its work just like it always does.
Give me one more clip of the nova
before the Earth closes again
like one enormous eye.

After LNAPRK by
Jean-Michel Basquiat 1982

His hat is always on, whether sun or middle of night,
every day lives by the same red circle, watching
the cows with their two organs, heart and stomach,
the bulls and bessies, slowly becoming mad,
making music with the banjo or rifle,
walking down the hill to school,
past the shrubs that grow in the shape of tiaras,
past the hot crow melting on the sidewalk, watching
the teachers write the same thing on the chalkboard,
numbering it something else, coloring over it,
eyes grow crazy and windmill, released
to the world and ready to eat their way
home, the blind luster of concrete,
the Douglas firs like tongue compressors,
the stars coming out, waiting the calm after
the calamity, waiting the moon.

Nutshell

Only the size of a walnut, a squirrel claw.

He was restless, I was
something unknown.

The shape of the skull in the ultrasound,
familiar pearl onion,
you, too, are life.

Never such a sound sadness throughout me.

In Portland this autumn,
the thunder shakes the rain out of its skirt
like a stork's blood bundle.

The landmarks call my name:
Something insane, something insane.

I'll never oatmeal-bathe him,
mittens over the nails.

If I deliver this child,
I might lose him in a crowd of liars,
better now to leave him in a cloud of stars.

I'll never show him the difference
between the American dream and way.

I'll never watch a bone
come through his mouth.

His undeveloped body,
sticking to me like garlic skins,
the limbs, sinew sack of maybe.

Every life is a gamble.

Soon the cherry blossom petals
will be swirling along the pavement
like pink wedding rice.

As if there are no mistakes.

December 9, 2009

In Norway, a strange blue light
in the sky grows into a white coil,
a spinning dervish opening overhead.
No one can explain.

A man walked into my clothing store
with a heart of dried blood
carved into his forehead,
speaking in circles like a sky spiral,
angry at the world for making all of this,
angry at the people, asking
for anything not dyed in chemicals,
anything not made in factories overseas.
He said, "Come on, this is God's time."

But I didn't come on.
I stood still in that despicable building
and watched him leave
and watched the girls laugh it off,
"How crazy the degenerates are in this city,"
still standing still
and thinking, *What?*
What have I done?

The Psychogeography Upstairs

Portland wags its tongue,
it licks my head and I am thrilled.
I smoke cigarette after cigarette
and the room fills with cumulus.
I keep my boots on,
and if I clear my mind enough,
time changes everything.

California, don't be angry,
everyone wants something for nothing.
I want to watch the city
transport its face and forge a name,
and still feel new and still feel the same.
I love it the most before it loves me back.
When I think it might learn.
It is a sick process that I crave.
I keep my boots on,
and if I clear time enough,
my mind changes everything.

There are autumn trees outside,
and no matter how I pray,
they will not stop the golden crumbling.
I dreamed I was an old king.
Everything I touched turned to fall.

The Firefly Ate My Glow and Left

I try to forget her in the bathroom sink,
I try to forget her in the curtain folds,
but the morning always grabs me,
an alarm of daybreak or its slow coma,
and I cannot forget her there.
In the space where I search for sleep's lost images,
I try to write her back to me.

Write her hair falling like silk worms,
releasing from the tree.

The chorus of keys types time out of the clock.
The sun puts morning on a stretcher.
The birds speak their siren,
an ambulance, my gentle defibrillator.

In my room without lightning,
the building earthquivers,
bending in the wind.
My bottle of wine draws me a bath
where time overlaps,
a Venn diagram
of night and morning.

Without her,
I am when flowers turn brown.

I am blank like a dead marquee.
Nothing is coming.

Strange Bird

God pulled me aside and explained the way he judges.
He takes the shell of a bird egg, places it over a candlewick
and his index finger heats up when it is near
the divination of a soul's intent and perspective.
So, ignorance is bliss, and children are most holy.

When he comes to me, his finger goes cold
no matter where he touches.
I let me know too much.
I saw every souls' eyes closed, blind-walking,
behind the dangling carrot, smiling, taking,
disgorging, starting over.

With the answers so close,
translation holds its hand over the light switch.

When he points to the palm reader,
his finger grows and burns red.

The tiny notches in my palm give my nervous blood away,
like the scars and dyes we pierce into our bodies.
The wounds we own to undo our wrongs.

The ink of my tattoo unravels out of the skin
and waves in the thin air beside my pelvis like a kite string.
The skin grows backward in time,
now even and pure like bread.

Sometimes forgetting is a form of baptism.

I go over and over the motions of flight
until the wind moves me,
an intervention in this madness.

To each his own, and for me?
I'll have everything.

Fluorescent

If somebody hits on you at the supermarket,
you should feel great.

Those are some very powerful lights in there.

One *Miss*, Two *Miss*,
Red Miss, *Blue Miss*

Once I get out of this head I'm sure I'll fit into
society quite well, and straight into a nice
codependent relationship where no one has their
own individual person, and we can forget ourselves
completely, and forget why we chose each other as
opposed to the other billions of people, because
what's the matter anyway – we are in California,
and the sun is out again today, shining its glitter all
over our obsession for each other – and the facts of
our love drown the spaces around us, which is just
to say that we know we could never love ourselves
as much as we love the other, our lover – and who
could blame us for loving every sun-dyed sleepy
second covering ourselves with each other because
when we are forced to remember, we never really
liked spending time with ourselves anyway – we
never really liked ourselves anyway – we never
wanted to think about it like that – we never signed
up for this reminder of ourselves. When the day
comes to a close, with its weighty darkness running
over the city like God's nosebleed, we never forget
to remind each other to *take a deep breath, baby*,
even if we suffocate ourselves in the process.

But this is just to say that if I could get out of
this head, I'd be able to tell you that I've thought
about you, considered the angles of your face and
the art that shapes behind it, considered how, to
be honest, I never thought you were the One,
considered how I might outgrow you – but even in

all this considering, I can't shake the colors in your paintings' backgrounds from the colors I dream in when I sleep alone under a blanket filled with dead duck feathers and wake up with my hand between my legs. I can't fight off my selfness when I leave folded poems like prizes at the bottom of your cereal boxes. I am exactly how I am, and sometimes I don't listen to a word I say, but bid myself farewell into my head, and let my memories of you cry themselves to sleep because I wrote you a note to try to tell you I miss you and it came out, "One miss, two miss, red miss, blue miss."

Erased

The poets I know
are biting their cheeks.
Their tongues button down
in the slick bed between teeth,
their eyes are a fourth of an inch deep
and trying not to do anything.

Once, we were blood
everywhere, the darkness
at the end of the tunnel, apocalypse
coming down the aisle to read,
building a bonfire to heat the room.
Once sparks flew out of our mouths
and we didn't call it spit.
We read like every human heart
spoke a language universal as neon.

The poets I meet
write poems about their dreams,
walks to the market, or over a bridge.
They don't want to hear about Victoria's cancer
making a chalkboard of her body,
the stillborn baby softly slipping out
like a sausage from the casing,
the birds and fish wearing slickers of oil
on the shuddering ocean,
or how the position of the sun
makes you sadder than anything.

My church has divided.

The terrible wits, brain-wigs, are trying to wash off
the kind of stain that comes out of me.

What we tried to build between the heart and the mic
is a song being forgotten, a palimpsest of feeling.

Here:
I have a recurring dream,
where my eyes won't open
more than just a tiny slit.

Versus[*]

The way I see it, there are now only two ways to live. When we are happy, and the women are sweet, with stomachs like cutting boards, and the boys are young Adam's apples, and the joy of our lives fills us and we are not compelled to move so much as lay around, or stare off at something lovely, not thinking at all how lovely it is, not thinking much at all. In this life, we roll over the earth because it is the same on our backs as on our bellies. We hold the pen above paper and forget why, because we know we have nothing to say.

Then there is the way to live where we are terrified, uncomfortable, and the women will not be mothers or even pretend to harness the hobgoblin or the real animal monsters, and the boys drool more each night, and their cries arrest the head, pack the ears like infection, and the nights grow so large that they howl and snarl and the stars are no longer pinpricks but shining fangs pointing downward. In this life, we pound our fists at the earth, frightened by what is coming in these heavy abdomens, too misshapen to rest on each side of our bodies, afraid of our unevenness. When we want to write is all of the waking time, which is every hour, but the wisest one has gone and hidden all of the pens, because when we get our hands on them, we are the most expansive fury. If we get a chance, our hands are the blades of jackhammers, mining ourselves a grave into which others can fall.

Each day we choose which life to live.
Either the bliss that drills a hole in our torsos,
leaking the art and words we have to say,
or the stillness that hardens over us like an eggshell,
our writing hands weaker than the embryo's beak.
We are trying to break apart.
We are trying to write our way out of this.

*(After the novel *A Plague of Wolves and Women*)

Secret Pages II

Since he only loves the small of your back
because it's helpless, the tears peel down your face
like fruit rinds. Close your mouth when you cry,
we can see your whole wet feeling,
hear it smack against your tongue.

At night, the naked branches poke
the meat of the sky like a fork,
and your mouth shriveling to a silent
petal, goes to hold its secret still.

Wings Earned

I wanted to open in myself,
at the end, when the feathers burst
from her shoulder blades,
the way the house coughs out
a moth into the night.
I wanted to grow up in the flap
and flutter that raises us higher
until the world fits into our vision
like an eyelash,
and we see life entirely,
the beginning, the end.
I wanted to find myself
grounding above it all,
and tell you how I cried
at the line she spoke
about how important the body is,
how I don't feel that way,
how I'm going to have to
learn the hard way.

I wanted to explain that
if we close everything into the mind
like a bag of goldfish,
we start to understand.
In the moment,
a man untangles a girl from his barbed-wire fence
while his Rottweiler drools uncontrollably,
a child is starving and singing
godsongs in the Ethiopian rain,
a man learns to swim on his fifty-second birthday
to save his wedding band
from the amethyst floor of the lake,

a mother burns the white lily on her son's casket
into her mind's eye until it blurs with tears,
a middle-schooler makes a part in her hair
where a bleach blonde streak grows out of her birthmark,
a wedding band continues to sink,
grandma falls asleep with her eyes partly open.

I wanted to tell you
about how we hold memory of the beginning,
but it's the final part of the pinch
that makes the blood bubble up,
the last clip that spoils the trick of our skin.
And still we pray to keep the end out of sight.

No matter how we speculate,
we can never fully anticipate feeling.
It is a judgment that only comes in the flesh.
A life sentence.

Deconstruction Trick (for Victoria)

I.

Cancer has a white way about it, a trick
like the presence of every color
creating blankness.

II.

The tumors shrank from her chest,
like snails dragged from salt.

There are holes now,
viewing gulfs displaying the bone,
large enough for a grenade to nest inside.
One lung filled with water,
one leaking from the chasm.

War can kill a place.

III.

Her husband tells her
what lovely end is coming.
No more pain.
"No more pain," she echoes.

Her heart is alive like a starfish.
The whites of my eyes
can barely turn on.

I will be dancing at her funeral.
Keeping time, keeping time,
keeping time, keeping time.

Lines Like Bees, Like Ghosts

I wake up still drunk, wine scabs on my lip, steady
stumble to the cafe, and I pick the seat at the
outside table right next to the grumbling homeless
man. My mind is muttering to itself just like he
is. It slices the lines of the book of poetry between
my hands, and then I'm mouthing and breathing
the words of Frank O'Hara – sometimes we lose
ourselves, the streams between conscious and
unconscious blur together and suddenly the rain
and the river are the same thing and I can't make
out the shore. He's waving his arms in the middle
of the street and still rambling as my pen makes
underlines in the book, and then the man takes
his seat beside me again and says softly, "This is
your book, of your poetry." My eyes start to sweat
because he's right, it is mine when I breathe it out,
this is what happens when I wake the words, when
I stir the dead.

Two months ago I met six-foot-tall dimples and a
mouth to match my own. We talked about what god
we pray to and how everyone in the city shares the
weather like a story we're all living together. He
went north and I daydreamed of telling him to take
that ring out of his lip and put it on my wedding
finger, that I only have one muse and she lives in
a red mess in my chest – if you want to know how
to fix me I make more sense in the dark, and in
the morning the sun will be a huge bell through
the window, a car alarm that we have no response
to but try to drown out with our own music. Even
though he went north to make the mountains

purple, I still think about him. The final star in
the constellation, pointed like a compass – this is
what happens when I hunt ghosts, when I stir the
dead. How can I stop believing there is meaning
everywhere when the trees in this park lose their
wings like tearing hundreds of bees. God, say all
that is hard to say. Give me something before
you take it away. Wake his words and give me his
vibrato, it comes in heavy shakes, an earthquake
that rocks me to lullaby.

Letter to Anne Sexton

Dear Anne,
My head is a bucket of cirrus.
Most nights I fall asleep to spinning walls,
and nightmare of those same walls
turning over like rocks
to show the worms
and sow bugs underneath.

My typewriter in the corner,
covered by its glass museum case –
and I think of the season you left us for,
hot or cold,
hell or heaven,
maybe I'll travel to you.

Remember when I could brush
the darkness off my shoulder like lint?
Now I am the color of an oil spill
and believe that God walks
in silk slippers down singed streets
where tired voices yell for him
and he forgets his name.

Motivational Speaker

Be who they need you to be.
Put your pants on.

Two Crows

The second time you took me home,
I woke in your bleak, white bed
and told you of the nightmare,
pulling flies and maggots out of my ears.
You drew my head to your chest
and said, "You scare me all of the time."

Yesterday a pair of crows seemed to
follow me around the morning.

This poem is for the lovers
that disappointment has surgically altered,
for those whose memory lays them down nightly
on their beds like an operating table.
This poem is for the blood that taught itself
only to run cold and anesthetic.

For years I've been acting like my wrecking ball heart
is someone else's lost marble.
For years I've been acting like my heart is a daffodil bulb,
only able to bloom once before it's killed by winter.
For years I've been acting like my soul
doesn't cry its eyes out,
and laugh a hole in the wall like a cannon backfire,
when I notice the simplest sky has its tips dipped in gold,
and spills out that never-ending confession,
and swallows the moon like communion.

Someday I'll push my tongue past the pews of your teeth
so that we can finally find a church to belong to
when our mouths meet.

That night you said it was strange
how we both have an affinity for crows,
you asked me not to wear perfume so that when I leave,
I seem less like a woman, more like a ghost.
You said you believe you understand what happens
when your body goes home to the earth
and the rest of you, home to the wind.

This is for the simple hearts that take poems like horse pills,
for the ones who welcome their dying day.

I thought of you yesterday,
when a couple of crows seemed to follow me
around the morning.

They seemed like they could've been you and me,
because they hardly ever pair off like that.

Like a Broken Window, Held With Tape

We don't know what to call it,
all of the half bites of burger still stuck to the plate,
and the yogurt going sour under the tiny fridge light bulb.
We couldn't even finish the single
pint of eggnog before it turned to stucco.
Our leftovers, mostly procrastinated trash,
as half a bottle of wine turns to vinegar,
and everyone is drunk when grandpa comes out
of the room he's sort of quarantined to.
He's in his bathrobe again, the whole terrycloth open,
the sash tied and just naked besides
the white stripe of linen across his stomach,
he's talking too close to my face,
saying I have beautiful breasts
and looking at them and asking me to give him a kiss,
like I'm a hen he's asking to give him an egg.
The dishes are cleared and scraped into waste,
we all look pregnant and switch to brandy,
and then grandpa's leaning in, cross-eyed at Michael's lips,
explaining his wife had a tilted womb and in order
to conceive, he had to enter from the rear –
this and dessert, none of us can swallow.
Feel the heavy cream rising up
like some backwards avalanche.

We want and want and want one thing,
until it is all we have to spit out.

Red House

The house is full of lovers who wake in pairs,
arms and legs unfolding, Escher puzzles,
blurring the lines.

From where God sits, they are framed
in a garden of dandelions and tall grass.
The morning opens their eyes like blue jays.

The walls are thick with nonresistance,
voices carry like underwater whale calls
as the pairs make love in turns.

Each one of us holds a clock in our chest,
encased in a city we've just fallen in home with.

What I want from him are countless things,
laughter that explodes like a startled flock,
that song to come through like the long awaited
overthrow of my jeans and heart.

In the space of daybreak
I don't know I don't know
him yet.

From where God sits,
the death of one thing is also its rebirth,
stars can only give way to a grander one,
an immense sun, dawning over his shoulder,
turning the house from shadow to red,
like a beaten mouth in love, opening to say amen.

Letter After Franny and Zooey

Franny,
I understood your feeling of God.
I wanted to lay down with you
each time you would faint.
I wanted to offer you soup
I knew you would refuse.
I wanted to lay down my life,
and read that story for you
again and again,
until you died,
pale in my arms,
next to the bleached book pages
of some simple story you loved.

A Pairing of Opposites

Let's cradle each other like bats,
soft light draining through the cracks
where our wings overlap.
I want that black shelter,
I want that shell back.

I want you again in the time
you started an argument that lasted for hours
until you got horny off my rhetoric,
and told me I'm a genius and
let's go to bed.

I want you back in the rain,
in that orange scarf,
you kissed me
and touched my rib with your thumb.

Come home to these walls
painted with my veins and DNA.
I want to take Polaroids of you,
tap you over me, over me,
like a fingertip on a wristwatch face,
then push you off, cold-shoulder.

You and I are mostly equal,
like medicine and poison.

Sheer

I.

Dear Prom Date,

You made my dress from fabric
we found in a warehouse.
Then the car died when we were scrounging
the thrift shop for your tuxedo shirt.
The payphone ate our only quarters
when we tried to call for help.
My love for you has only become
more confusing.

II.

More strippers I meet are married.
I wouldn't know from their diamond rings,
but because they tell me when
I ask them to come to my house for money.
But they are still never growing out
their pubic hair or wearing pantyhose.

III.

The whale has a heart in her head,
even when her mouth is a snarl
and she seems to be showing her teeth—
Remember, whale teeth are thin
like guitar strings, strung too tightly together.

IV.

Tonight, he says, I love you and I love our life.
I say, I love you more than I love our life.
And every time I look at the cat,
as easy as a run in new stockings,
I can see when it will die,
while I am well and washing under my arms,
and still watching the tree growing in the yard,
and finding the small animal's shed fur
around the house for many years after.

Study of the Skull*

We're not very old,
but the fluid might clog,
and the spine may fail.
The brain is a quacking chick
above the pumping chambers,
always something
to gas and beak about.

Our vertebrae form a stairway
what ails us learns to climb
and finally injects the hen,
making her mute and caged,
the plaid-lined scalp
cozies around the fowl,
until it's time to sleep
without end.

*(After *Notary* by Jean-Michel Basquiat 1982)

Anatomy

I blow a gum bubble,
the size and shape
of your scrotum.

And I pop it.

The Room Next to Yours

The room next to you is loud at the worst times,
barking at you when you come home late at night,
moaning and breathy in the coldest waking hours,
pounding stomps with the chunk of stripper heels.
The room next to yours is rented
by someone you've never seen.
Sometimes you imagine her, an old widow,
who loves her little dog so much,
her whole apartment smells like dog,
dog hair in the shoes, dog sweat on the couch.
Sometimes you imagine him,
the one in the room next to yours,
as a frat boy who keeps a girlfriend
like a schedule, like a mustache.
Sometimes you imagine her, as a Pinocchio doll
that comes alive at night,
hair waving like octopus tentacles,
lips heavy on everything in the room,
entertaining her guest for the evening,
skin moist and the waft of cherry scent
on her few items of clothing,
especially making your mouth feel like one thing tonight,
even with your lips in two soft pieces, still feeling alone,
even with your hands' twin company,
both clasped under your jaw, settled on sleep,
but each swooning song and gasp from next door
becomes its own melody of exclusive love,
somehow worse than the silence you make by yourself,
somehow worse than the nightmare
you were already having.
The room next to yours is there to remind you
that the one thing you can't be

is the grease when you need to be the wheel,
that there is something missing
in the worn dips of your shoes,
wherever you're going, you want to get there
before you get there.

Then this week, the crossword has the shape
of a smiley face in its dark spaces
like God is laughing down at you,
and you leave the apartment to have a cigarette
just as the room next to you opens, to reveal
that the person living next door is exactly like you,
looks like you and fumbles with the keys like you.
You nervously nod at yourself and make your way,
down the same staircase, and quietly dismiss
all of the terrible things you thought about yourself,
except maybe the way you longed for you,
slowly wringing your fists, trying to remember
trying to remember.

Too Many Things Are Occurring
for Even a Big Heart to Hold*

The rabid nights when the moon
shines behind the eyes
and they inflate to the mirror.

The star jasmine would hum to me
and I would rest my head
into the honey brush of tree.
I swore to my friends
that the stars were pointing
at me from their crystal balconies.

Here, I am the thumb of a puppet,
some bottom lip, a shadow
of our most common action.

What I have to shine to the stars
are these nails, digging,
digging, digging the sand,
breaking through
to water.

*(Quote from an essay by W. B. Yeats)

Freefall Flight

Tonight, I feed myself winter.
It sticks to the tongue, bitter putty.
The spoon's in my mouth
when I go to the window.
Weren't parrots supposed to be flashing
among them in a fury of wide open wings?
A parade of life to remind me
that an entire world exists outside of this.

Then I walk to the window and fall out.
And it is beautiful and I am happy.

The Tape That Held Your Voice

There's dried blood on more
than one corner of the bandages,
like a ravaged bushel of mulberries,
and she's still so pretty,
outlined in white tulle,
with a bouquet of ice,
and a train of damage in her track.
Maggie's bleach blonde head wrapped
in thick inches of gauze,
like someone mummied her mind.

She met a faded friend
to have whiskeys, after some distance.
She knows there's a reason for that space
but the spirit moves through the glass
and before you know it a ride
on his motorcycle through Hollywood
looks like the light bulb that just turned on.

Without a helmet or leather,
she grabs his frail waist across the Sunset Strip,
past Crazy Girls giving love from table tops,
Grauman's Chinese Theatre,
tacos and the grey donkey,
and plunges five meters from the bike.
Maggie's spindly limbs cover her face
as she cannons.

She finds consciousness,
her hands are ruined ribbons.
Ant trails of blood crawl out of her skull.
Somehow she stands and calls for help,

but her voice is a tape unwinding,
a dream where you try to scream and can't.
She waves her splintered arm at cars passing,
stops a woman walking by.
The woman is standing up straight
but her shadow is crooked.
She pushes Maggie away,
she thinks this is inconvenient,
or she's late to a concert,
has to move her car before a ticket,
or all of this entertainment
makes Maggie look like a morbid movie
none of them paid to watch.

No one stops.
An ambulance
doesn't arrive for an hour.

Painting Hancock Park #5

And all of a sudden
I'm dreaming again,
in these ghost shadows,
playing across the paint,
thin as carbon paper,
that labors you over the day.

Looking at *Hancock Park #5*
I start to cry by the way the blossoms
shift in phases to disappear,
becoming more and more
like the transparent boughs
that give them away to the sky.

It is my favorite hour, the most painful,
when I let the light get the better of me,
and my eyes turn to tiny aquariums.

I dream in that space,
while the lavender phantom
hangs in the next room,
listening to us have sex and sweat.

With the sunken sun,
I stop watching the sky like a fishing line,
and ask you to close every door.
Because my eyes are doors,
not windows,
and I cannot promise
to feel like home.

Sometimes My Feeling Does Not Happen to Swell Into Words[*]

Tornado in my throat,
doesn't mean sentence or even solid thought.
Hurricane behind the eyes can pass
in the train on my way from work,
when the four-year-old and I notice
that we are wearing the same boots,
one week since I dropped the child from my womb,
and wish she was mine,
and the older man facing us a few seats away
glancing back and forth from her tiny boots to mine,
from her smile eyes to the tears welling up,
a head only a fraction of my head,
a hand only a finger of my hand,
a tide rises in my oceanic chest,
the train keeps on moving, escalating the bridge,
taking the people home from work,
the stops are called in their usual order,
the little girl and I look each other in the eyes,
and my feeling does not swell into words.

*(Quote from Marilyn Monroe's diary)

After TUXEDO By Jean-Michel Basquiat 1983

What you think you own
has only accepted to live among you.
Sometimes living is just lying around.

These days, crowns are see-through,
looming far overhead.
Everything is a math problem,
calculable and naked.

You think you are king,
and all that you own
is obedient like arithmetic,
but you have a throne made of chalk,
and your belongings are white wisps,
your people, the shadows between.

Your followers will fall off
like common denominators,
and what you own will dust out.

Then comes the rain,
like nails scraping downward.

Ex-Girlfriend

Alone in Virginia
with three dreams of violence
and my own death.
In the morning you call to confess.

Virginia is for lovers
of triangles, or the crick in a duet.

But I can tie a bow with one hand,
wash my own spine.

When I write her down,
I make her eyes even smaller,
like beach glass, I grind them to sand.

I fill her mouth with thorns,
flip her hair to one side.
All the whispers fall out.

When I write her,
I lay her down as my slave,
ingest her pheromones
and invade her
until I am closer and deeper inside
than sex has ever been.

Virginia eats me alive,
and I try to rot inside her.

Bridge

Drawbridges rise up and keep me from whatever pigeon
and sidewalk and leaves I'm not trying to turn.
When I cross over, the heroin chic offers to buy me coke,
or whatever I need to feel good.

He waits for me to fall asleep,
watches me with my hands balled up between my legs
because the window's open, no blankets. As I drift off,
my voice is a balloon deflating, a flag coming down.

When I wake, there is the promiscuous needle,
the ugly spoon with its drop of residue, a drying swamp,
a few corners of paper towel crumpled
where the brown blood hardened.

He's standing there, a fern in his own house,
he's the bar of soap with dirt streaks,
the inch of coffee molding in the green mug.

I drive home and the entire city is re-colored,
the mothers and sons and lovers and just friends
are more crawling across the street
than walking to or from a place of purpose,
more shriveling from the sunlight
than eating or digesting it.
Now more than ever the ocean is a thing to become part of,
not a thing to make part of oneself.

He lays awake, fights the urge to feed the sea into one arm,
imagines stepping outside but knows what usual moon
with unmoved craters, decides to skip the whole thing,
primes the fang, torches the branding iron, lowers the bridge

and just as many horned demons as pink elephants
walk over into his vein, making a circus of his mind,
and they all march out to the sidewalk,
and finally welcome the day and the aching sunrise,
the bleached fronds and the weathered roadway,
and the girl who escaped or mistook
the elation that laid so simply and clearly,
boiled and ready when she was there in the house.

Hand Painted Sign
(for Margaret Kilgallen)

There was no question
between the cancer and the baby,
like two perilous portraits,
the agony and joy, thespian masks,
they work in unison, tandem,
not believing in divorce.

She feels sick and drops the brush,
there are too many paint drips to wash off,
she is smaller than this thing inside her,
she returns home to replace herself,
and somehow, all she sees are profiles,
and the world is easier to let go.

Marriage for the Black Orchid

I came to California in the dead of winter.
The pollution makes it eighty degrees.
I came here to throw you a wedding.
This is a marriage for your mouth
and the lie you always tell,
kissing cousins.

I don't mind that my chest is a cast
that sets my heart like a broken limb.

Watch your napping heart,
the one I mistook for a black orchid.
It might die, my sweet,
some things die in their sleep.

In Los Angeles, I become a human cage:
frightened of what I know I will do.
The city is obvious, turning all the lights on.
No coat closet to hang my darkness in.

I will return home to the pouring weather,
the trees blossoming in bursts
like electrical fuses left out in the rain.
Our sex was a storm I never meant to survive.

For C. Noelle, to Whom I Wish Wings

Not one for division,
but pushed into this bleak corner,
she turns to grind these pills
to make her air.

She rips the plastic gloves,
puts the left on the right,
the right on the left.
*Bring the separation to
a crossroads*, she thinks,
make the differences the same.

The dye fucks up
and now her hair is blacker
than she can discern
from right or wrong.

What is a seed in a field of soil
compared to a seed in a pile of seeds?
We'll get to that blankness
when we love enough to leave.

Familiar Me

I am confused by my apartment's masque,
its color codes in black and white,
how blood is heavier than oil,
how red is darker than purple
in the shade of things.

Haven't you any idea,
the ghost you leave in your wake,
after you wake, after you go,
the faint spirit leading or following me,
from the bed, to the couch, to the kitchen.

This loneliness is bruise-colored,
and covers me like plague.
Remember we would write,
the stars becoming unfaithful,
the time of day ripping us apart
from the eyes down?

Took a nap again
and woke up without my solace.
The mailbox is empty
no matter the day.

How glamorous to lock
myself in this studio,
and type type type
all over this keyboard,
and make make make
the poembabies
all night long,
like bonus pornography.
The typewriter
is always up for sex,

with my fingers all down
its skinny spines,
smooth rows of vertebrae.

I wish things were more disposable.
The ashtray's to your right.

The City Spits Us Out

I try to warn you about the city
I had to cut out of my skin,
that seeped from my ears like altitude,
my compulsion to the pen
that searched me into hideaways,
where shadows craved me,
cornered my carbon copy—
And you!
Trying to tell me
only darkness can love me like that.

Datura

With its petals pointed,
I chew it into me,
the tips of each sword
sticking their way
to all of my vacant craters.

How it is so like the skin of an apple,
though four or five grams
sings a eulogy.

Pupils dilate to rabbit holes.
Through the demon's jar,
Catalina Island is more defined
than the lines in my hand.

Night rings its tepid bells,
I swallow the golden trumpet,
switch places with the girl in the mirror,
until she becomes a new creature.

I pluck the poisonous moonflower
and wonder why it is never explained
that the simplest trick
for the magician to do
is disappear.

Lovesong Snares

My leotard makes me squirm.
It's really too hot for wine
but I can't help myself.
The painter, whose hands fit me
like ghosts of glass slippers,
is calling about a weekend.
I trip on my words
and everything in the room.
My body temp rises and my feet
belong on a dock or a plank,
somewhere I feel consumed,
where I think, *My God...*

Maybe I'm not the one
you waited for your whole life,
maybe instead, the one you overlooked,
the one crying on the typewriter keys,
the one who scrawls without technique,
dances herself into bruises,
and writes you love poems
that sound like funeral dirges
for your open eyes that end
when our sex closes them.
As an antecedent
to the thousand miles between us,
when we meet, the walls bend without drug,
colors in the room bleed
like finger paint on funhouse mirrors.

In the track of your scent and movement,
only gravity and my own hands,
I fall faint beside the cat and candle.
For now, this heart is a cake of rosin
waiting to oil the strings inside you.

Quicksand ℳ*e Under*

I send my simple mouth.
It's all I have to give.
Build a nest.
Pluck the branches.
Pluck my blood fortress for dinner.
Get me out of the air's way.
Get the mosquito needles
to float right through me.
Get the twigs back in the tree.
America builds a nest
around its head and ears.
"No screaming here,
no screaming there."

God, bless the children of the world.
I have always heard you love them.
Where are their nursery rhymes?
And their missing limbs?
"Up here, they are
holding my cold glasses.
They are flipping my book pages
as I yawn them to sleep.
The angels have almost
forgotten their songs."

Down here,
Norman Mailer's youngest words
cling on the page in front of me.
Norman, draw my body naked in your book.
You are eighty-four this year
and I can't think of a better place to be placed.
Draw a caption under my belly.

Draw lines around my eyes
because they're always open.
God, don't make me stronger,
I want to always cry at moments like these.

God, get me out of the air's way.
I'm collecting what's left
of my porcelain and heading for the sand.
Get it to learn my head to toe.
Get it to spin me, a cyclone,
and scatter me like broken art over the city
because I can't think of a better
place to be placed.

Our House

From the porch seat,
the gloss of the neighbor's dark window
reflects the glow of our kitchen light.
Our curtains are missing,
and I watch your silhouette make tea.

The rain is a soft swarm of bees around me.
The cherry pops out of my cigarette
and lands by the dead fly on the deck.

We are a limited snapshot.
Your illuminated frame stirring.
Four brittle legs neatly folded over
the fly's onyx, skyward belly.
The smoke derailed,
unable to keep its train of thought.
Our kitchen window,
a shining sun bursting from
the next building's
black brick galaxy.

I go inside.
The house is empty and
you haven't been here in years.

Sometimes I am the fifth wall of this bedroom.
The chaperone in the constant date
between the floor and the closed door.

I lay out the charcoal and
light a fire on the hardwood.

An Eclipse of Moths

One woman is late to board with two tiny children;
I give up my seat for them, move to the back.
The steward slips me two miniature bottles of vodka,
my own little glass family.
Let us all lean in one direction.

From inside this airplane, as the cars grow toy-like,
so does the curl of your mouth.
What you look like from nine miles away, I can tell now,
the ivory stones that will someday become of your body,
how there's some end we're all nearing,
some light that makes us feel like valleys.
Let us all face in one direction.

There is a wild moth, trapped on the flight,
flapping anxious, then soft-landing.
Those dust screens, pressed tightly upright,
turn the whole creature to a speck.
Sometimes when our wings are the most open
is when we seem to disappear.
Let us all fly in one direction.

My small window like a missing tooth
gives way to a shrinking world,
I can lonely imagine, all the stinking hookers
you bought in my wake, before you knew
this ship could come home,
before you ate my sweater,
unraveling it from one loose thread
like a whisper of moths, feasting.

How love is the animal that destroys, shapes,
but it is also the cloth that wraps us together.

As I Tell Her That We Own[*]

We brush the cat's tail,
slice the mold out,
wipe the chalk over,
slip on the leather gloves,
live our salad days,
keep pocket change for the poor,
the spirit-tormented,
the psychically graceless.

At times I remember
when the grass was not token,
when the trees were not events,
when the tide folded at its own origami,
that we come back to the earth.

Darling, there are places here
who remember us, falling into our art,
by the sea in the ruthless sun,
me, drawing natal charts and horoscopes,
you, knocking castles with one toe.
All that we owned was a day on the beach,
but then, all the plates and papers
and books and kisses, nightmares
of children, of crocodiles, dimes
we kept for ourselves, and empty glasses,
plants that can't grow through the concrete,
wine bottles, and clothing, socks,
painted asphalt, the freeways signs
that won't lead home.

*(Quote from a poem by Leonard Cohen)

Disappearing Act

This is our disappearing act,
we take one step forward,
two steps back.

In a world that turns to change,
we twist to mist,
but not to rain.

As the last song graces,
the earth we knew
forgets our faces.

Carrie Seitzinger is the author of the chapbook *The Dots Don't Connect* (2004). She graduated UC Irvine (BA: English, Poetry Emphasis). Her poems have appeared in *Poor Claudia, Sparkle & Blink, DASH, Mosaic, Unshod Quills, Housefire*, among others, as well as various anthologies. She is the poetry editor of Small Doggies Magazine, and currently lives in Portland, OR.

Find out more at www.carrieseitzinger.com.

Acknowledgements

So many thanks to The Small Doggies Family, and the Portland Literary Community.

Thank you to the Orange County Poetry Community and those there from the beginning, very especially Michael Roberts, Jason McBeath, Greg Austin, Melody Marie, Jaimes Palacio, Buzzy Enniss, Derrick Brown, Dan Rubiano, Ben Trigg, Steve Ramirez, and Maggie Wells.

Thank you Shenyah Webb and Rick Klaras for support I could build a house on.

Thank you, Lidia Yuknavitch, Matthew Dickman, Rachel McKibbens, and Derrick Brown for connecting to these poems.

Thank you to Maggie Foree for your patience and wine while editing with me.

Thank you Maggie Wells for your hot moves with a red pen and your sister heart that matches mine.

Thank you to my family for such love.

Thank you to the men and women who broke my heart.

Thank you to Anne Sexton, Jean-Michel Basquiat, Frank O'Hara, J. D. Salinger, Tori Amos, and Margaret Kilgallen whose minds, art and music have reared their way into these poems.

Mostly, thank you Matty, for changing my life without changing me at all; for your honest commitment to my work without sacrifice of your own; and for inspiring me with your paintings, your words, and your fighting, gentle heart.

SMALL DOGGIES PRESS

Artful Fiction & Poetry
For Lovers Of The Written Word

———⟫•◦•⟪———

Small Doggies Press supports, defends and publishes the most beautiful, challenging and artful prose and poetry that we can find. We believe that the author has all the power, and our job is to create a context within which they, and most importantly their work, can flourish and find the intelligent, curious readership that it deserves.

Small Doggies Magazine is a home for writers and readers, a place to exchange ideas and to cultivate dialogue about whatever is going on in contemporary culture. Sometimes this is straight forward, sometimes that conversation will be jumpstarted through satire. If you feel that you want to join this conversation, then you should find us online and send us a note.

Both Small Doggies Press and Small Doggies Magazine are divisions of Small Doggies Omnimedia, LLC, an Oregon Corp.

Visit Us Today:
www.smalldoggiespress.com
www.smalldoggiesmagazine.com